PAINTING DREAMS

ERICA ROBIN

SAINT MEMORY

WWW.SAINTMEMORY.COM

This book is dedicated to all the dreamers

STORY

I use my art as a personal form of therapy to help heal myself as well as others. I come from a family of turmoil, addiction, abandonment and depression. I have lost 3 people who were extremely close to me to suicide. I believe one of the reasons why so many people are unhappy today is because we have lost our connection to ourselves, to nature and to one another. I intend for my art to serve as a bridge into consciousness that we are all one and connected. I strive with every finished work to invoke feelings of empowerment within oneself and the divine connection that unifies us all.

I always had a love for art, but I was never serious about it to the point where I had to do it. Well now I feel like I have to. There is no other choice for me. I must express myself, or die. As dramatic as that sounds, it's the truth and art really has saved my life. If it wasn't for art, I would be dead... just like my best friend, brother and stepdaughter. Why is art so important?

I believe that we are all creators. God is a creator. When we are creating, we are at our highest level and we are closest to God in this way. Expression is key to staying sane in an insane world. It was the key for me. Whatever is your dream, you can achieve it. I am living proof. I was able to turn my pain into to something beautiful. I want others to know they can do the same.

I would describe my style as a combination of surrealism, visionary, and fantasy. I use parts of my life and what I've gone through to tell an interpretive story. Sometimes I start with a specific theme or narrative. Other times I let it unfold naturally as I am painting. I call my process intuitive flow, meaning I use a feeling and energy to carry me through the painting to the end result. I paint with oils on birch wood panels and usually work on several bodies of work concurrently.

Art gives you emotions. People are always trying to numb emotions but its the opposite of what we should do. Emotions are power, they are energy... it's what makes us human. If used in the right way, emotions can be your superpower. They can drive you to do amazing things.

Art can heal you with the certain emotions you feel from looking at an image. It can bring a nostalgia from past, present or future. Imagery is very powerful, eyes are the windows to the soul. Most of it is subconscious, its all subliminal, we don't even know what it's doing to us when we are looking at it. That's what is so powerful about art. My hope is for my own art and voice to heal people.

I am the Dreamer, you are my Dream.
You float through my mind, face unseen.
My breathless wish is for your touch,
I yearn for your kiss, I need you so much.
I can see you through my minds' eye,
Your sparkling eye's shine like a bright summer sky.
You're not even real, nothing is what it seems,
You touch my heart and bleed into my dreams.

My beautiful dream you have my soul,
I need to inhale you to make me whole.
Just give me your lips but for a time,
I'll dream a world where you are mine.

Because you live... I dream...
Spread the love... and peace will follow...

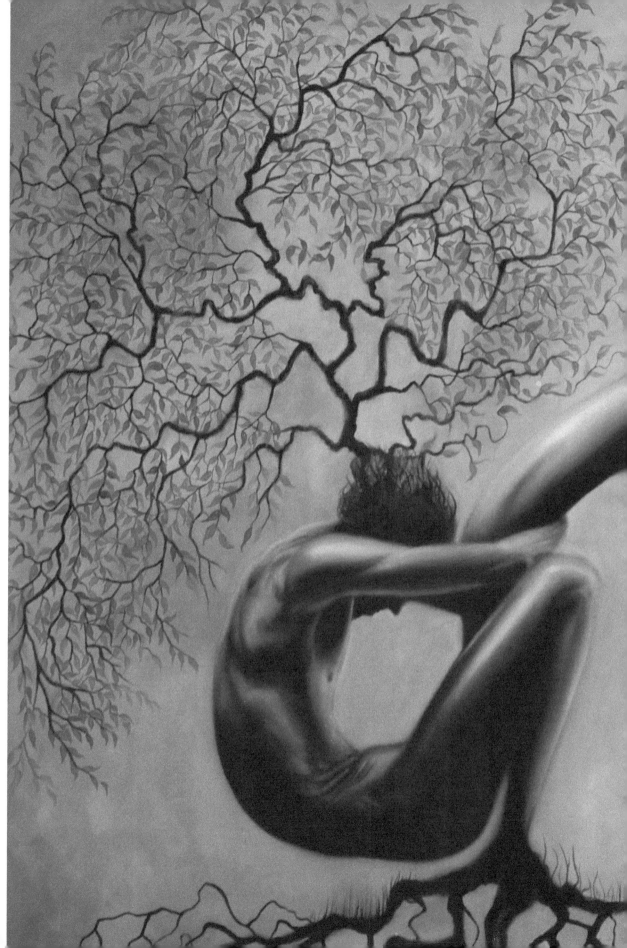

I love you doesn't mean I want you for myself. I love you means I want to do whatever
is in my power to help you flourish in every way in whatever way possible;
spiritually, emotionally, mentally and physically. I love you.

You are the root of my spiritual growth and the
mirror of my deepest desires, needs, and fears.
You reflect back to me all of my inner shadows,
but also my deepest beauty and greatest strengths.
We grow together.

Love is not a feeling or enthusiasm, but a skill.
The story of how they painfully learn from love.
The understanding of oneself, the other person,
and learning to communicate despite
the gap that exists between them.

The best love is a love that awakens the soul.
A love that plants a fire in your heart
and peace to your mind...
that's what you are looking for...
that's what you have found forever.

I am so grateful to know pain and love,
for both have the most beautiful dance together.
Love causes pain; pain causes love.

*There is nothing more beautiful than when your
feeling like the world is trying to pull you down,
and someone is there to remind you that the
Universe and they are here to help hold you up.*

Spiritual growth is never ending...
we can never stop growing closer to God,
learning lessons and making changes.

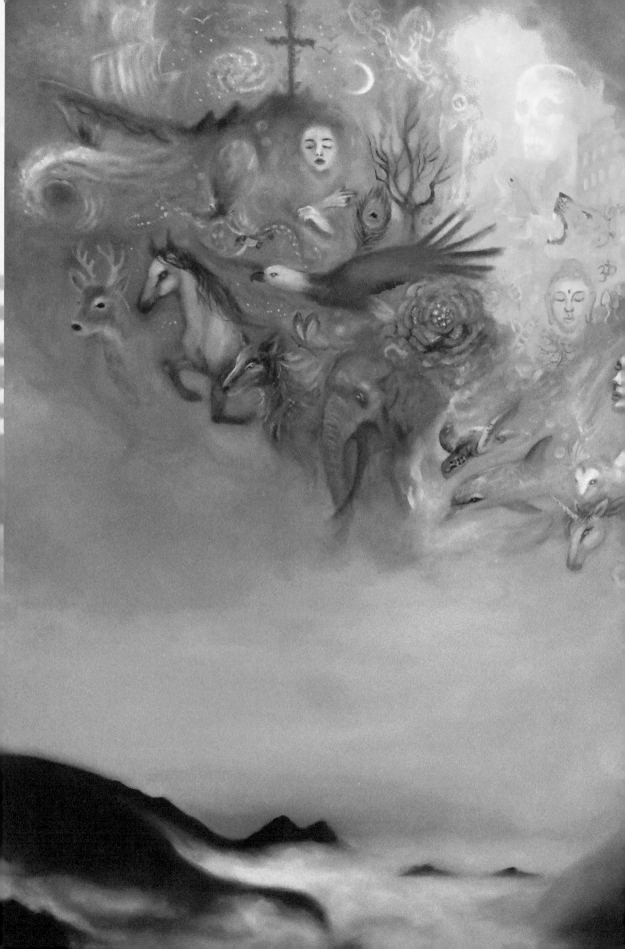

It's ok if your dreams haven't become a reality yet, God has a better imagination.

I've been searching for my twin flame my whole life,
only to realize my twin was inside of me all along.

Erica Wes

We live on a blue planet that circles around a ball
of fire next to a moon that moves the sea.
Miracles, miracles everywhere!

You are beautifully and wonderfully made.
You are perfect just the way you are.

Erica Wexler

My soul has gone through the depths of hell
so that I may heal myself and others.

Don't let society or anyone else ever tame your wild and free nature.

We sprang from the tree of life. When our hearts touched, the spark caused new worlds to form.

To love and be loved by you has opened a portal
of creative imagination, reminding me
that we are all limitless...

Love is the answer.
Love is how we got here.
God is love.

*"In the name of my Higher Self and the Higher Self
of my beloved twin flame, I call to the Holy One for
the sealing of our hearts as one, for the completion
of our holy purpose. Wherever my twin flame is,
cut them free. Free us now to fulfill the Divine plan.
In order to unify us and draw us together for the
healing of this planet. We thank you and submit
ourselves to your Holy will. AMEN."*
~ *source unknown*

Wherever you are, wherever you go,
I'm here to dream with you.

"We're just two lost souls swimming
in a fishbowl, year after year."
~ Pink Floyd

Creator of chaos in this life and other realms.

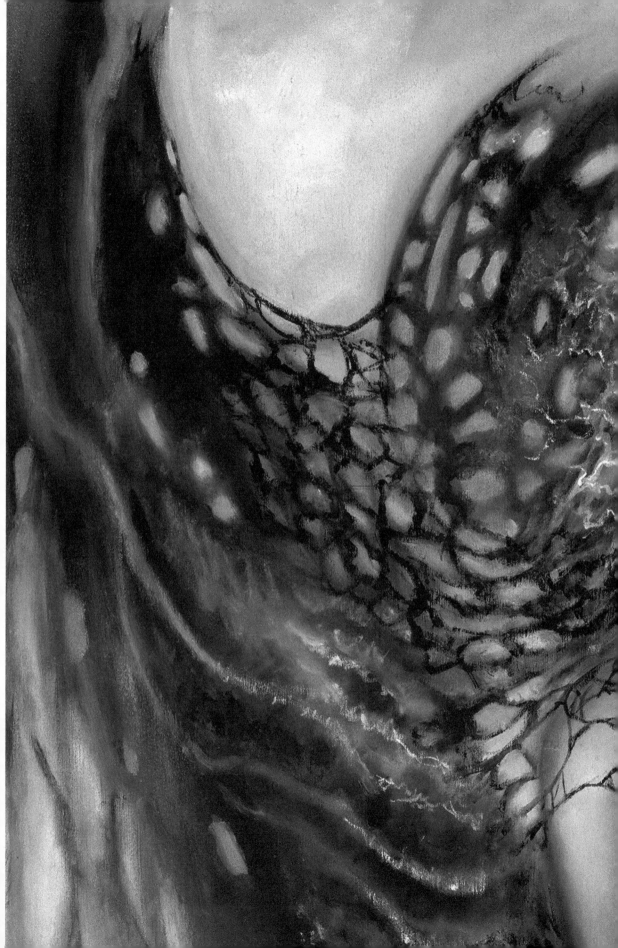

We all have the power to either affect or infect the world around us.

Wild was her nature.
Soft was her heart.
Sweet was her soul.

Does the gravitational pull
of the moon affect our moods?

Now is the time to free your mind and soul.
We have reached the pinnacle.
We are coming out of darkness into a lighter era.
Where more of humanity will start to remember
they are in an amnesia and realize their magic
they had forgotten so long ago.
Time to Wake Up.

Sometimes you wanna just die
from a broken heart.
But somehow,
you keep on living.

Warriors are not born nor made.
Warriors create themselves
through trial and error,
pain and suffering,
and their ability to conquer
their own demons.

Cosmic duality, sets of two opposing and complementing principles. As above, so below.

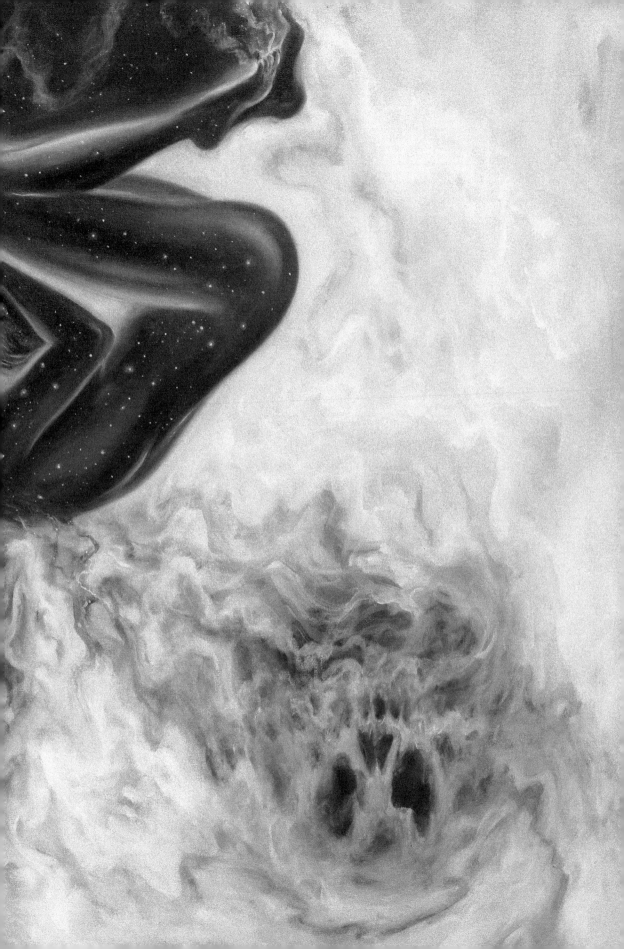

The Sun loves the Moon. He dies for her each night so that she may shine.
And she only shined, because he was there. Fated to wait for each other.
Finally a passionate touch, that was needed ever so much. It was so intense,
they had to commence, to go back to await, the next day of their fate.

The world was on fire
and no one could save me
but you.

Some can stay in your heart but not in your life, but that's the perfection. The heart has no concept of time or dimension... it's an endless bounty, readily available to those who are needing to nourish.

May my heart be an overflowing river of nectar
for those in need to feed.

Resistance of the soul to its destruction
by a deranged world.

Nature is thy medicine.
Envelope it around you
as much as you possible can.

*Cintamani grid around the planet is one of the
major tools for manifesting the planetary light grid.
Whenever a Cintamani stone is planted in the soil,
a huge angelic being is anchored in that spot,
creating an energy vortex miles in diameter.*

Erica Robin

A Spiritual teacher is a person who assists others,
one who transcends all suffering by leading
them back to themselves.

Never loose your wild.

Love has love's best interests at heart.
Be love and others will find their way home.

Hello mystery.
Don't bother to explain.
Love will split you open,
into light...
into the Universe.

Her medicine feeds the world.

*I wanted to tell you I love you. I wanted to tell you
I'm so grateful for you. But somehow you don't
want to hear these words. I want to say it's ok,
but I feel the stagnant loneliness that is in my heart,
and I cannot ignore the pain. I sit here in my
authenticity knowing I have done everything I can
for now to call in my true soulmate. I am here
looking into my heart wondering why I have to
feel so alone. I see so many beautiful empowered
women wondering why love left them. Or
wondering why it never came at all. Despite the
beautiful moments in between, we share this
underlying heartache. You can't rush what you
want to last forever dear heart.*

Love and spirituality are inseparable... for there can be no love with a selfish spirit.
When spirituality grows, so does the capacity for love.

Let's ride this wave of dreams and see where it takes us.

Erica Wexler

Different perspectives,
different worlds.
Similar admiration.

I feel the closest to my creator when I am creating.

Soul family are those that assemble around you, not connected by race or blood, but by energy and essence. They bring love and support at the perfect times and understand and share the same mission for being here. I am grateful for my soul family.

You're taking me to some kind of magical place.

God will reward your courage.

Most days I am strong enough to handle the
beautiful treachery of life on my own.
Today I've lost my sea legs and need to be held.

Paths that I go down.
Trails that I've crossed.
I ponder sometimes I've gone off trail.
Other times I'm confident of my path.
Whatever path I'm on is the right path
as I am lost nowhere.

I am the ocean, the vast expanse of water that sustains all of life, to that you can fall into. I can either soothe you with my calm waters or drown you with waves of emotion.

Be attached to nothing. Then you will have everything.

As a woman goddess warrior high priestess,
we flow with the moon.
She speaks to us in our sleep
and guides us through her whispers.
The serpent slithers through the darkest of spaces
to find our deepest truths,
waking us up to our true power.

For every dark night is a brighter day.

Thank you God for giving me the greatest gift of consciousness for enlightenment. You truly know what you are doing in every intricate part of existence. There is a miracle happening at every moment. We just need to break the veil in order to truly see the sea in front of thee. For thine is a vessel of fate that awaits the heavens. This is the journey of the soul, this roller coaster of light... riding into the night.

*Many of us have forgotten the magic that exists
within our own hands. The human hand is blessed
with its own supernatural intelligence; they have
the power to harm, hide, hammer, hasten
but most importantly, they can HEAL.*

We don't see things as they are, we see things as we are.

Erica Robin

Ahoy to the greatest adventures in life.
You'll find at times
it may give you some strife.
It is not only gold
and silver you treasure,
but having each other,
no one can measure.
So sail away to the open sky,
just spread your wings,
and let's fly high.
Where we are going,
we don't quite know,
that's part of the thrill,
so enjoy the show.
So remember dear friends,
life is pure magic.
If you don't already know,
then that is just tragic.
A cosmic voyage is calling thee,
ride the wave and set yourself free...

Fierceness is showing vulnerability when
suppressing emotions is easier.
Being present when you are presented with vapidness.
Giving with no expectation of receiving.
Trusting without knowing the outcome.
Giving the world all of your heart and soul.

My artwork is me and I am free.

Don't bottle up the magic that is inside of you.

Erica Wexler

Even though our love is ever changing,
it is forever present.

Love is not a feeling we are waiting to experience.
Love is not feeling emotionally high all the time.
Love is the kindness and compassion
that your offer to yourself and others.
Love is the support of the experience
throughout the duration of any feeling.
To the ego, love is a super arousal.
But love is not a feeling.
Love is the harmony
that glues ALL feelings together.

Art gives us a glimpse of the other side,
the ephemeral unspoken truths,
the hidden seeds to grow new worlds.

I once was on the verge of dying.
Having reached the highest level
of my ability to Endure pain.
Until God sparked a flame of light
inside of my heart.
Now I spend most of my time healing.
I am a miracle grasping at the galaxies,
collaborating with the cosmos.
I Live to show you the Art
of turning pain into beauty.

If we've lost our connection to nature,
then we've lost our connection to ourselves.

*Pursue what sets your soul on fire
with reckless abandon.*

If the doors of perception were opened, everything would reveal itself as it truly is...infinite.

Erica Wex

CONTENTS

Publisher Contact:
hi@saintmemory.com

product id #3693697693771111
www.EricaRobinArt.com
www.saintmemory.com

If you have any issues with quality, delivery, or content and
would like to report it directly to the publisher, please visit
feedback.saintmemory.com.

FIRST EDITION

CPSIA information can be obtained
at www.ICGtesting.com
Printed in the USA
LVHW070020101121
702881LV00008B/183